A QUEENS

Love Story

LaShawn Sam

Printed in the United States of America

ISBN: 979-8-9986404-6-9
Library of Congress Control Number: 2025922309

Cover Design & Interior Layout by Purposely Booked Publishing

Edited by LaShawn Sam

Published by Purposely Booked Publishing | www.purposelybooked.com

Dedication

I dedicate this book to anyone who has ever experienced a traumatic event or events that caused a ripple effect of life challenges, including abuse, rejection, low self-esteem, self-sabotage, drug abuse, and alcoholism. I want you to know that you do not have to hold on to those burdens; you are and will be an overcomer. You can move from trauma to triumph.

To my husband, James Sam (my knight in shining armor), and my children, Janasia Sam, Justin Sam, Jordan Sam, and Josiah Sam, thank you for loving me and standing with me through my journey. It's your love for me that pushes me forward every day. Thank you to my mother, Yvonne Haynes, who never gave up on me, even when I gave up on myself. To my siblings Antoine, Keenan, and Avonna thank you for always looking up to me and loving me even through my pain. In loving memory of our daughter Jaiden Sam.

Uylessees Sept (My daddy, the first man who showed me what it meant to be loved) and Johnny Haynes (coolest dad ever).

Special thanks to my leaders, Bishop Cranford and Dr. Sandra Davis, for always pushing me to be great, and Elder Deborah Durham author and playwright who coached me during the writing of my book.

Disclaimer

By no means do I claim this book to be the solution for total recovery. I suggest that if you have experienced a traumatic event, please seek professional advice and help to begin your healing journey.

For me, my recovery began when I was introduced to a man named Jesus! 2 Corinthians 5:17 King James Version: Therefore, if any man be in Christ, he is a new creature: old things are passed away; behold, all things are become new.

Table of Contents

Lashawn's openness and heartfelt compassion immediately resonated with me from our very first conversation. I was looking for faith leaders to join a training on how to identify and support victims of domestic violence, and Lashawn's genuine desire to help others heal from their pasts and reach their fullest potential stood out. This book is a powerful example of that commitment—it's a story of triumph over trauma.

In the pages of this book, the reader is invited into a profound journey—one that is both heartbreaking and uplifting, raw and redemptive. It is a story not just of survival, but of transformation, where the darkest experiences of abuse are met with incredible strength and resilience.

Lashawn bravely opens the door to a past filled with unimaginable pain, yet in doing so, also reveals the extraordinary love of God that heals, helps one reclaim their voice, and rise above the very traumas that sought to define them. Through every chapter, we are reminded that abuse may fracture a person's sense of self, but it does not have the power to destroy the soul. There is light in the darkest corners, and this story is a beacon to those who may still be trapped in the suffocating grip of their own struggles. It shows that healing is possible, that triumph can be achieved, and that hope is always within reach—even when it seems most distant.

This book is for those who have experienced trauma, those who have witnessed suffering, and anyone who believes in the power of resilience. It serves as both a powerful reminder of the pain abuse causes and a celebration of the strength that rises from it. Whether you are walking through your own journey or offering support to others, these pages will touch your heart, change your perspective, and inspire you to believe in the possibility of transformation, no matter the odds.

Sharice Potts, MPA
Domestic Violence Advocate, Community Outreach Leader

Trauma is a profound disturbance and alarming experience that removes the mechanisms to overcome a person and causes significant emotional and psychological stresses. Recovery after trauma is complex, and it is an individual process. It can take a few months or years to heal and face the lasting effects of the experience. With proper support and treatment, many people can overcome trauma in their lives.

Introduction

When I was a kid, I was never afraid of the dark. My friends always talked about the boogie man, who would come out at night and lurk in the dark. I was such a tough cookie that when bedtime came, I would jump in my bed and be out like a light. Sweet and peaceful dreams would follow. I could watch a scary movie and be okay. I was never afraid of the boogie man!

Chapter 1
Summer Summer Time

The sun was so bright, school was out, and I was so excited because the next school year I was going to the 4th grade. But I was going to enjoy my summer with mommy and my little brother. I wondered what we were going to do this summer. In the past, we would travel down south to Bamberg, South Carolina, to my Granny's house—she was my daddy's mother. But sadly, mommy and daddy were no longer together, so our trips down south came to a stop. I hated that those trips had to end.

Mommy didn't seem happy. I felt she was missing something in her life. She was a single mom raising two kids. I guess she needed someone in her life. I remember she had a friend who would come by. He was so nice, but honestly, I think he didn't want to be with a woman who already had children. Don't get me wrong, he treated us well. He had a motorcycle, and every time he came over, he would take us on rides, slowly up and down the block. They were really good friends, and I guess she needed someone in her life. It looked like they cared about one another, but as time went on, we started seeing less of him. Then, I really don't remember seeing him at all.

Mommy seemed a little unhappy again, and I hated to see her that way. I loved to see her happy. Mommy was the smartest woman in the world to me. She always had a really good job doing secretarial work, and she dressed so nicely and was very professional. But something was missing. My brother and I hadn't seen Daddy for a while. It seemed like he just forgot about us. I really did miss him a whole lot. I wondered if he loved us anymore.

I remember looking out that big bay window in our house on 149th Street in Queens. Our house was really nice. Mommy rented it; it was a 3-bedroom, living room, dining room, kitchen. There were 4 floors: the attic, basement, main floor, and bedrooms upstairs. The attic was a full attic—it was huge.

Mommy was handling her business. She was working hard to provide for her children. I still missed my daddy. One day, I was looking out that big window. The only person I knew to talk to about how I was feeling was God. I heard he could help! I didn't know this God well, but I figured he could help me. I started talking to him, and I told God how much I missed my daddy. I was daddy's girl, but daddy didn't love us anymore—so I thought. This was my first real conversation with a God I did not understand or know anything about, but something deep down inside told me that he could hear me. Would he listen and help me? That was my question. I knew he was real; I just knew it.

Later that day, I was outside playing jump rope with my

16

friends. We loved to jump Double Dutch, and I stopped in the middle of jumping because I saw a man walking up the street. He looked just like daddy. I began to run up the street, "Daddy,

Daddy!" I yelled, but the man kept on walking as he waved and smiled. As I got closer, I realized that was not Daddy. I could see in the man's face that he felt so disappointed for me. The hurt on his face, because I was hurt, was priceless. He smiled and walked away. My heart was broken that day. One thing for sure, it would not be my last broken heart.

I became so mad, I stormed in that house and went to that window. I looked up at the sky and yelled, "WHY DID YOU TRICK ME LIKE THAT???? THAT WAS NOT DADDY."

That evening, I went to bed early. I didn't even eat my dinner. My poor little feelings were hurt. I was so disappointed. I turned off my lights, put the covers over my head, and cried myself to sleep. My room was pitch black, but I was not afraid of the dark or scared of the boogie man, so I just continued to let the tears flow. That was my first conversation with God, and it didn't go as I expected. I thought he created these mystery miracles. He isn't real!

Chapter 2
Out of Nowhere!

Time went on. The leaves on the trees began to change colors. The season was changing, and life went on. I was now in the 4th grade, and school was going well for me. I made a lot of friends, and life was good. My teachers were nice. Mrs. Crews was my history teacher, and my music teacher was Mr. Shelton. Those two teachers I remember because they were so hard on me. They always called on me, and I always got caught talking. Everybody else was talking too—why do you always call me out? I thought. Sometimes people can see something in you that you don't even see in yourself. Maybe I will be somebody one day. Jeremiah 1:5: *"Before I formed you in the womb I knew[a] you, before you were born I set you apart; I appointed you as a prophet to the nations."*

One day, my brother and I were at school, and a bully was picking on him. He was only in the first grade. I had to protect him, and I did just that. I balled up my fist as tight as I knew how and just went to swinging. My arms were flying everywhere. I didn't know how to fight. Shoot, I never had to fight before, and I'm sure I missed more punches than I got in, but I sure was going to protect him at all costs. I lost the fight, but at least my little brother was okay, and he learned that you have to stand up for yourself.

Out of nowhere, Mommy had a new boyfriend. I guess they dated for a while, but my brother and I didn't know or see him at all. Hmmmm… I wonder! Maybe Mommy doesn't want us to meet him yet. The day finally came when we met her new boyfriend. He seemed okay, and she seemed happy. They dated for a while, then he made himself at home. Mommy moved him in. A short time later, we were told that Mommy was going to have a baby—a little boy. My brother and I were excited. We were going to have a little brother. We were going to be one big happy family—Mommy, her boyfriend, and us.

After Mommy had the baby, things began to change. I would babysit my two brothers all the time. I was still young myself.

Mommy and her boyfriend hung out all the time—they partied hard. I remember his sister, who my brothers and I considered our auntie, and her children, who were our cousins. They would come to Queens and spend the weekends. They lived in Far Rockaway, which was a part of Queens. The whole weekend was one big party—the kids were upstairs, and the adults were downstairs. The only time we went downstairs was to eat or go outside; other than that, we were upstairs.

I remember the music blasting at night. We would be up sometimes until like two or three o'clock in the morning. They used to come upstairs and tell us to go to sleep. We would pretend like we were going to sleep, and as soon as they went downstairs, we were back up. Question: why do parents think if they party, blast music, and talk loud, we can sleep? Duh, the music's too loud, and y'all are loud—we can't sleep. So, we just played.

The weekend passed, and Monday was here—no school for us. They were too hungover from the weekend to go to work and for us to go to school. We would take turns visiting each other. There were times they would come to Queens, and sometimes we would go to Far Rockaway. Mommy's boyfriend did not have a job. He didn't work, but she did. She would get up in the mornings and go to work, and he was just home. I never really paid attention to all they were doing and what was going on, but they were drinking and drugging, which became the norm for them.

Chapter 3
The Boogie Man Is Real!

I told you I was not scared of the boogie man. Well, that changed when the boogie man decided to come visit me. I had my room, and my brothers had their room. We had a set bedtime every night: 9 p.m., because we had school the next morning. The routine was to pick out our school clothes, take our baths, and say our prayers. You know the one that all kids say—It goes a little something like this: "Now I lay me down to sleep, I pray the Lord my soul to keep, and if I die before I wake, I pray the Lord my soul to take." Goodnight!

My room door was closed, but I heard it open. I was so sleepy I didn't really pay it any attention. I closed my eyes and went back to sleep. Suddenly, I felt a tug on my covers, then they were pulled off. I jumped up, and the boogie man tried to hide. I lay there shaking and terrified. What did he want? Why was he coming in here to bother me? Why was he in my room? His cold, clammy hand reached up and touched me. I jumped. I was so scared, I just laid there, numb. I closed my eyes real tight. The boogie man began to rub me in places no child should ever experience. I didn't know or understand why this was happening to me. This continued for a couple of minutes, but it felt like hours. The boogie man stopped and then he left.

My mother's new boyfriend was the boogie man, and at night he would visit me and do bad things to me. I thought I was a tough cookie, but I learned really fast I was weak and scared. I kept quiet. I did not tell my mother what was happening to me because the boogie man told me not to tell. She had a baby with this man, and she seemed to love him, but for me, I felt all hope was lost. I no longer had happiness. I no longer had joy. Truly, I felt like life was over for me. I needed my daddy. Where was he? He was supposed to protect me. I felt so disgusting, dirty, and ugly. It was the worst feeling ever. I kept asking myself, "Why is this happening to me? Was it something I did? Was it the way I dressed?" I started wearing baggy clothes. I started to just put on anything. I didn't care how I looked. I dressed how I felt—UGLY. I wasn't styling my hair; I just didn't care.

The first part of the verse in John 10:10 says, "The thief cometh not, but for to steal, and to kill, and to destroy."

That's exactly what was happening to me. I was being destroyed. I was damaged to my core. Things only got worse. The Boogie Man gained some confidence. He not only showed up at night now, but he also showed his ugly presence in the daytime too. Sometimes, I hated coming home from school. I would walk home and take the long way. Sometimes, I would just walk around, trying to avoid going home. I knew what was waiting for me. I wish I could walk around until it got dark, then Mommy would be home. I was too young to keep walking around those streets, so I had to go and face the Boogie Man and let him continue to violate and traumatize me. The Boogie Man now went from just touching my private parts to getting on top of me. He made me lay there while he thrust himself inside of me. The feeling, the smell, the fear—it was so much for me. I felt nauseous, like I wanted to vomit. It was vile and nasty. I just couldn't understand why this was happening to me. I became a totally different little girl. I hated myself because of the way I looked and felt. I hated myself for not fighting back. I began to act out in school. My grades were up and down, mostly down. I was now a totally different child. I hated myself for not fighting back when he would hurt me. The little girl who did not know how to fight was now fighting all the time at school. I didn't know how to express myself. I was only 10 years old, feeling like I was walking around carrying the weight of the world on my shoulders.

It was too much for a 10-year-old girl to handle. People can tell when you're in a weakened state, and they started bullying me at school, so now I had to deal with all that was going on at home and the abuse at school. There was no escape for the little black girl from Queens, NY. I had no joy, and I had very low self-esteem. I hated myself, and I felt the way I saw myself— everyone saw me that way. The next day, I woke up to go to school, and I was so drained. I was depressed, tired, sleepy, and sad—all wrapped up together. I gathered enough strength to get ready for school. I cried the whole day at school. I felt so alone and so broken. DOES ANYBODY SEE ME? All those adults at school—teachers, guidance counselors, the principal, the cafeteria lady, or security guards. DOES ANYBODY SEE ME? I really think that in the education system, the adults who are caring for the children should be trained on how to recognize certain behaviors in the students.

When I got home from school that day, to my surprise, Grandpa was at the house. I watched my favorite show and ate some good food. Grandpa lived uptown in Manhattan (Harlem), but he would sometimes travel on the A train from Harlem to Queens to come visit.

Grandpa would always bring us Bun from the Jamaican bakery in Harlem when he came over. It was a little taste of happiness. I still was feeling sad. I had all kinds of emotions and crazy stuff going on in my head. I wanted to tell my grandfather so bad what was happening to me, but Grandpa was no joke. I didn't want him to catch a murder case, so I kept quiet!!!! That night, bedtime had come, and Mommy and The Boogie Man were not home. I slept peacefully that night, but I kept waking up. I sat on the side of my bed, thinking to myself that everything and everybody would be better off if I wasn't around.

Remember, the enemy's job is to steal, kill, and destroy. He plays mind games with us. He began to talk to me and tell me that I would be better off dead, and you know what? Once again, I did not fight back. I agreed with him. I went into the bathroom. The steps I walked from my bedroom to the bathroom felt like freedom was ahead of me. All the pain, all the hurt, the rejection I felt, the self-hate—all would soon be over. I would be Free! I looked in the mirror in disgust. I didn't like what was looking back at me. I closed the bathroom door, opened the medicine cabinet, and grabbed the first bottle of pills I saw. I opened the bottle and took the whole bottle of pills. I walked out of the bathroom and went into my brothers' room. I kissed them goodnight and whispered, "I love you." I went back to my room and laid down with a smile on my face—no more hurt and no more pain. I drifted off to sleep. To my surprise, a bright light woke me up! Where am I? I looked around, and everything was so familiar. Ughhhhhhhh! I'm still here in my room. I became angry with God again. WHY GOD? WHY DID YOU LET ME LIVE? I guess He is keeping me for a reason. I sure would like to know what in the world that reason was.

Psalm 10:17: I shall live and declare the works of the Lord! Who, me? I am a nobody.

Chapter 4
Short Lived!

My behavior in school was getting worse. I acted out so badly, but NO ONE paid attention. I started hanging out more with the kids who were skipping school, smoking weed, drinking, and smoking Newport Cigarettes. I did not try any of those things; I just hung out with them. As my time was coming, though, I was experiencing things at 11 that opened me up to a whole new world. Who skips school in elementary? The streets of Queens, NY, were calling me. There was a park called Baisley Park where we used to hang out—not often, but at times we did. There were stories told of children being murdered at that park and thrown into the pond. That didn't scare us from hanging out there, but I bet you we were gone before dark. They decided to build a new park on 150th Street. It was right around the corner from where I lived on 149th Street. That was the new hangout spot. No matter what, we always made it home before the streetlights came on. I was now 12 and in the sixth grade. I decided to tell my mother what was happening to me by the man she loved. I knew this would crush her and break her heart, but I had to tell her what was happening to me. I was so broken; I couldn't take it anymore.

I thought if I told her, the sexual abuse would stop. It will finally be over. Mommy confronted the Boogie Man, and he had the nerve to tell her a bunch of lies. His biggest lie was that he wasn't thinking clearly. Remember, I told y'all they used a lot of drugs and alcohol. He told Mommy that he smoked some angel dust (embalming fluid) and that it caused him to hallucinate. How long does this drug cause you to hallucinate—years? Come on, man! He said he was out of his mind and did not realize what he was doing. Yeah, okay! Mommy seemed to believe his lies. She talked to me and told me his story and that it would never happen again. Mommy said to me, "If it ever touches you again, he will be outta here faster than you can sneeze, faster than you can say 'Achoo!'"

Weeks went by, and the Boogie Man had not shown up. I started to think maybe it was the angel dust. Was I trying to convince myself so that Mommy would be happy? A few more weeks went by, and still no sight of the Boogie Man. I was good— nope, not really. The damage was already done. I didn't like me. I was asleep, and I heard my room door open. I began to wrap the covers and tuck them tightly underneath me, crossed my legs, and held them closed. I did not want him to violate me that night. This night the boogie man wanted something different he made me give him oral sex and he did oral sex on me that was it for me I hated myself even more. Dude I was 12 years old are you serious? The next morning, Mommy was in the bathroom getting herself together for work. He had already left for work— he finally got a job. I walked into the bathroom, frail. I felt sick. I was so broken. As my eyes swelled up with water, I looked up to my mother in a soft, shaky voice and said, "ACHOO!" Mommy said, "What did you say? "I said, "You said if he ever touched me again, he would be outta here faster than you can say 'Achoo.'" Mommy called his sister. I will tell you what their conversation was another time. Mommy called the police. They picked him up from his job, and he was arrested.

Chapter 5
Graduation Day!!!!

I'm graduating out of the sixth grade today. I can't believe I made it—or were they just trying to get me outta there? Truthfully, I think it was a little bit of both. Daddy was at my graduation. I was so happy to see him. We would see him now and then; sometimes we would go stay the weekend with him. One thing I noticed, though, is Daddy would drink a lot. He was an alcoholic. It seemed like my mother's drug use had increased some, but at least the Boogie Man was gone, and we saw Daddy more. I still felt so alone in the world. I had to find my way. How was I going to do that? I had no confidence in myself at all. I hated me. I did not feel pretty. I felt so ugly. I just did not have any clue what to do with myself. How do I start to like me? Will I ever begin to believe in myself? Nope, I don't think so. I'm just worthless. I will never amount to anything.

Chapter 6
Elizabeth Blackwell JHS 210

Trauma is real, and if it isn't dealt with, it'll seep into every part of your life! Even though I wasn't being sexually abused anymore, the damage had already been done. By the time I was in Junior High School, all I did was fight. I was such an angry little girl, and many times, I cut class and just walked the halls. Do you remember earlier when I told you that when I was younger, my friends were drinking and smoking? Well, my time had come. I smoked my first Newport. I choked so bad on that first puff, but the second one was easy. Soon, I was smoking all the time. I didn't have money to buy my own, so I would take my mother's leftover cigarettes out of the ashtray. Sometimes, I would go into her pocketbook and steal some from her box. My first sip of Old English beer in a 40-ounce bottle—I was 12. My mother had no idea what I was doing. Mommy decided in my second year of JHS that we were moving out of New York City. I guess she wanted a change—maybe a better life for us, a new start for me and my two brothers.

Chapter 7
You Can Run But You Can't Hide!

We moved to a little town called Grit, Virginia, and we moved into a mobile home. It was small, and I did not like it. It looked like poor people lived there. It was a trailer park, and I wasn't used to this. I kept saying to myself, "I'm not gonna like it here." I'm a Queens girl, and she got us down here in the middle of nowhere—no stores, nothing. Well, looks like we better get settled in. It was a new start, new people, and maybe even new friends. Well, my hopes of making new friends were shot. People really didn't like me, not to say I may have not been likable. My demeanor was straight NY—I didn't care if you said something outta the way; you would get dealt with. I was so defensive about everything. The thing is, in the small area and the surrounding areas, those people all knew each other. They stuck together, so it was the country kids against the city girl. No one really got to know me, and honestly, I didn't want to get to know them either. Ughhh, why didn't she just take us home? We don't belong here. There were bullies at the high school I went to who tried me, but not this time. I got a point to prove to them that I'm a city girl, and y'all not gonna play or try me. I had a fight almost every week now. I was labeled a troublemaker, but I didn't start the fights—they did. I just finished them. I remember I broke my hand because I broke this girl's nose. Yup, I was just standing up for myself. No one else would, so I did. I vowed to myself that I would never let someone do anything to harm or hurt me ever again. It got to a point where I didn't even argue—I just went to fighting. I started being the one to throw the first blow. I went to my first adult club at the age of 13. There were teens and adults there, and my mom took me. I met a boy there who became my boyfriend. He was already an alcoholic. I dated him for a while. Things in the South are different from up North. After a while, I got tired of him. He was always drunk, so I broke up with him. We dated for almost a year. He would come to my house crying to my mother, and she would listen and then talk to me. I didn't have time for his drinking problems; I had my own stuff going on. Finally, he stopped coming over.

My grandmother lived in South Jamaica, Queens, on Linden Blvd and 126th Street. She was from the Caribbean and of Jamaican descent. Kingston, Jamaica, was where she was born and raised. Mommy received a call that Grandma was sick. The school was getting ready to let out for summer vacation. I would be going to high school in the fall. I would be in 9th grade, so that summer, we took a trip back to New York to go check on Grandma. We didn't realize how sick she was until we got there. Grandma was diagnosed with pancreatic cancer. No one knew she had cancer—she never told anyone she was sick. I remember going to the hospital, and I didn't even recognize her. She didn't look like the strong Jamaican lady I knew. My grandmother was the best cook ever. I remember her making us porridge for breakfast. She would make ackee and saltfish with dumplings and green banana. She used to make the best soup—it's called cow cod soup. I used to eat it until I found out what part of the cow they used to make the soup (you don't wanna know). I had good memories of my grandmother. Mommy seemed to be okay. She was happy to have laid eyes on her mother. We stayed for a couple of weeks, and then we went back to the country. A few weeks later, Mommy got a call. I remember it as if it were yesterday. I had gotten in trouble at school, so I knew when I got off the school bus, I was going to have to hear my mother fuss at me. But I was cool with that. When I got to the house, my mother was sitting on the porch smoking a cigarette. I thought she was waiting to discuss my trouble at school, so I went to talk, and that's when she said, "Shawn, I don't have time to talk about that now. Your grandmother has passed away." My heart dropped. The look on her face was so sad. She was heartbroken, and so was I.

A week later, Mommy told me we were going back to NY. I thought it was just for the funeral, but she explained we were moving back to NY to live at Grandma's house. Mommy's boyfriend was moving to NY too, with his country self. He was a little cuckoo, if you ask me. When we got to Grandma's house, all you could smell was mothballs. Yuck. I hate that smell to this day. All of Grandma's furniture was covered in plastic. No one—I mean no one—could sit in her living room on that furniture. Why do West Indian families' houses smell like mothballs and have plastic on the furniture, and no one can sit on it?

I had a conversation with my grandmother before she passed away. She said, "LaShawn, I have to tell you something." I was like, "Okay." She went on to say that Boogaloo— that was her nickname for my daddy—I had no idea what she was going to say. I would have never thought that the next words to come out of her mouth would break my heart. I was a daddy's girl. Nothing she could say would make me love him any less. I was waiting, my heart was beating so fast. She said, "He is not your real father." I had just turned 14. I was like, "Come on, God, what next? Am I gonna be disappointed my whole life and live in fear of what's going to happen next? If so, why allow me to live and continue to be disappointed? Why did my mother and who I thought to be my father lie to me? Why?" One thing Grandma said before she died that has stuck with me was, "To him, you are his daughter, no matter what." With tears in my eyes, I asked her, "Who was my real dad?" The answer she gave was shocking. It was my mother's real close friends—they were like sisters. We called her Auntie. It was her brother. I was so confused.

Now I'm feeling like, why did my real father not love me? I began to let the devil talk to me: "No one can ever love you. You are unlovable." He began to say, "Why are you alive? You are a nobody. You will never know who you are." I hated my life, so I decided to take it again. This time, I took pills out of my grandmother's medicine cabinet and drank some liquor behind it. I knew for sure it would poison me. I went to sleep. I don't even know where my mother was, but I was home alone. I just felt a little woozy and dizzy. My head was spinning. It felt like the whole room was moving. I felt hot. I slept in my grandmother's old room. I went to the window, opened it, and let the air blow on me. I just sat on the floor, looked out the window, and cried. I fell asleep right there. I woke up sometime later and walked to the bed. When I woke up in the morning, I was so mad at God. Again, another suicide attempt, and you let me live.

A few months went by, and I decided to ask my mother who my father was. She acted surprised, like, "What are you talking about?" I told her, "Before Grandma passed away, she told me the truth." Mommy was like, "Why would she do that?" Mommy began to tell me the story that when she met Daddy, she was in a bar, already pregnant with me, and they started dating. He was older than her—much older—but that was okay. Mommy went into labor with me at 6 months. I was born premature. I weighed 2 pounds and dropped down to 1 pound. The doctors did not think I was going to make it through the night. The devil was trying to kill me even back then. One day, Mommy came to the hospital to see me, and Daddy was with her. When he laid eyes on me, he told Mommy, "That is my baby. Make a promise to me that you will never tell her she is not my daughter." Mommy agreed.

My biological dad was a very popular high school football player. He was offered scholarships to play college football. He and his mother came to my grandmother's house one day to talk over the situation. His mother decided that he was not ready to be a father, and he was taking that scholarship and going to college, so they would pay for Mommy to have an abortion. He was also dating another girl who was a cheerleader, but they were supposedly on a break. They were all in the same high school—John Adams. His mother expressed that if Mommy kept the baby, he would have nothing to do with either one of us, and that was just how it was. My grandmother had strong Jamaican beliefs and did not believe in abortion. She put him and his mother out of her house that day. He never looked back.

God always has a ram in the bush—he sent Daddy to take the place of being my father. I will always love my Daddy; no one will ever hold his place in my heart.

My high school years were beginning. I was going to the 9th grade. It started off pretty good, but I was dealing with so much. I was such an angry teenage girl. I went from an angry little girl to an angry big girl, an angry teen. I had low self-esteem, and I didn't like myself at all. It all started with the traumatic experience of being sexually abused as a child the seed was planted and then so many branches grew from that seed that was planted so many years ago. I could not shake the feeling of not having love for myself. I didn't care anymore. It was like, whatever, it was. My mother's drug habit was in full force for her and her country boyfriend. This was when the crack epidemic was out of control. I started feeling embarrassed in school because some of my friends were drug dealers, and she would purchase drugs from them. So, in my non-logical thinking, I was like, why go to class? I started skipping school again. I was in and out, though. Some days I went and did well, and some days I didn't.

One day, I was on my stoop talking to my cousin. She lived right next door to me. I saw this boy walking up the street. I asked my cousin, "Who was that?" She said, "That's Jimmy." I was like, hmmmm… It was love at first sight.

Chapter 8
A Queens Love Story

This is where a Queens love story begins: The butterflies in my stomach were on 100 as he walked up the block. He was on his way to the bus stop—he worked at McDonald's. Oh my gosh, he is so cute, and he's getting closer. I want to say something. How do I get his attention? I want to say something, but I don't know what to say. Think fast, girl. Oh no! He's about to pass my house. I was feeling good; I had just come back from uptown, getting my hair done at Ace Hair Salon. I had some fresh finger waves—I was cute!

Jimmy was dressed fly. He had on some fresh Reebok Classics with a gum sole, black pants, and a dark navy blue shirt with a design on it. But here comes that old devil whispering in my ear: "A boy like that isn't gonna like you." The devil continues to say, "You're ugly, you're disgusting. He wants a pretty girl with a nice shape. You're just skinny, dark-skinned, and have short hair." So I kept quiet.

Jimmy walked by. As he passed, I mustered up some strength, opened my mouth with a loud voice, and yelled to him, "Nice shirt!" OMG, that was so dumb. But to my surprise, he responded, "Thank you." I had to say something else, so I said, "Can I borrow it?" He said, "Yeah, you can." That was how our friendship started. Usually, I wouldn't approach any boys because my self-esteem was so low. All my friends had boyfriends; I wanted one too.

Jimmy and I began to talk all the time. We were cool. He

knew I liked him. That blew his head up even more—lots of girls liked him. The school year was starting. Summer was over! I met this other boy at school. I started making a lot of friends. I had a crew I hung out with at school. John Adams was the high school I attended.

As the school year went on, I started dating this guy from Guyana. He had a car and would pick me up for school and drive me home. My mother met him—she liked him, but she didn't like me riding in his car. I was only 14, a freshman in high school.

At that point in my life, I pretty much did what I wanted to do. When I didn't listen, she would put me on punishment. I didn't really care—I would deal with it, and then when my time was up, I was back outside! My boyfriend was a little bossy. He didn't like my friends and always wanted me to stay in the house. I was like, "Boy, please, you are not the boss of me." I began to develop an attitude. We would go back and forth, arguing because he was always trying to tell me what to do. He was alright, though. His family didn't really care for me. His family was from Guyana; my family was from Jamaica. At least I had a boyfriend.

The one thing about him was that he didn't really like to go out or spend money. He did occasionally, but it wasn't enough for me. My family was having a BBQ at my aunt's house, so I invited him. The house my aunt lived in now was the house I grew up in, where all the trauma happened. I had not been to that place in years. I thought I would be okay to go back there, but as him and I pulled up to the house, my stomach began to feel sick. I began to sweat, and fear came over me. My heart was racing. Wow, what was happening? Mental illness is real. I just started yelling at him for no reason. I didn't even want to stay for the BBQ. I told him he could leave, and I would walk back home.

I was taking all those feelings that I was feeling at that moment out on him. He didn't understand what I was going through, and I did not want him to know. Two weeks went by, and I didn't hear from him. I did call, but his mother always answered and said he was not home. So, I decided that was the last time I was going to call. Oh well!

In the meantime, Jimmy and I started hanging out more and talking more—just chilling. He would come and sit on my stoop, and we would hang out for hours. We'd walk up to the corner store, and he would buy me candy and snacks. We were just hanging out. Sometimes we'd buy lunch. We would get two 50-cent sodas and a hero sandwich. His favorite was turkey and cheese with mayo, lettuce, and tomato. We would share the sandwich.

One day, we were hanging out on his stoop, just talking. I felt safe with James. This was different. His name was James, but everyone called him Jimmy. I started calling him James. I never discussed my situation with anyone, but I felt I could talk to him. I had kept my secret to me, myself, and I. That day, I told James my secret. When I think about it now, I feel like I put a burden on James. Why do I say that? Because it was not his burden to carry. We discussed my mother's drug addiction and the sexual abuse I had been through for years. I told him how I was helping to raise my siblings and all I had been through. He was silent. He just listened and looked at me as I told my story.

I feel that at that point, James took on the responsibility of taking care of that little girl who was broken. He wanted to make sure I was good—he took care of me. I will explain how later. I felt so special in my own way. That was the day I really knew what love was. I fell in love with James. I felt he was the only one who really loved me for me. I knew my two little brothers loved me, but this was a different kind of love. I knew my mother loved me, but she was so busy doing her thing. One day, I heard some loud music playing outside. I looked out the window, and it was my boyfriend, the guy with the car, parked in front of my house. I was shocked to see him—I hadn't seen him for a while. I'm thinking to myself, **"Boy, bye! Why are you here?"** I went outside anyway. I talked to him from my gate. He knew I was over it, but I talked to him anyway.

I looked up and saw James, boy, in his yard. He kindly walked out his gate and walked to James' house. Oh boy, here we go! A few minutes later, James and his boy were walking up the street towards my house. I was stuck—I didn't know what to do. I just started laughing because James and them kindly walked into my gate and into my yard while I was talking with this guy. James and them were just looking at him.

So, James decided to interrupt the conversation. He yelled and said to the guy, "Yo, leave! Get away from here, and I better not see you over here ever again!" They had some words back and forth. James told him, "I better not see you come to this house, and I better not see you on this block!" I was so shocked. I was in love—he chased that guy away. I guess that was the end of him. Maybe I was gonna be James' girlfriend now.

I waited and waited. James didn't ask. It was July 2nd of 1989 when he finally asked. What do you think my answer was? **YESSSSS** (lol)! That day, my life changed forever.

July 4th, everyone had on their 4th of July outfits, everyone was throwing BBQs. It was like 85 degrees outside, and here comes James to my house. I was glad to see him, but he had on all black, and he had a hoodie on. I'm saying to myself, **"Why does this boy have on a hoodie?"** We talked for a moment, and then I snatched the hoodie off. Your boy had a hickey on his neck, and I did not put it there. I told him to leave—get out of my yard. I was so mad and hurt, but I did not show it. I acted like I didn't care, but I did. Being hurt was the norm for me, so I just sucked it up.

46

I had not seen James for about two days. On July 6, 1989, he came over and laid it on thick. I forgave him and took him back. I will never forget 7/6/89—that's the day my life changed forever.

I mentioned earlier that when James and I had that conversation about my trauma, he took on the responsibility of taking care of me. He did. I never wanted for anything—he was always there. James and I went to two different high schools. He went to August Martin, as you know, and I was in John Adams.

For some reason, James kept popping up at my school. James spent more time at my school than he did at his own school. He was there making sure I went to class. I questioned, **"If you're always here, how do you have time to be in class?** You're concerned about me being in class; you should be in class." Life was good. James was no longer working at McDonald's; he had a new job where he was making big money. Every day before school, he would leave me $20 or more in his mailbox so I would have money for school, and he would take me shopping every two weeks. I had new sneakers, jewelry, and clothes all the time. He bought me my first pair of door-knocker earrings and a two-finger gold ring.

I would save some of the money James would give me and buy stuff for my brothers. James brought them stuff too. At this point in my life, I felt I was grown and pretty much doing whatever I wanted to do with limited parental guidance. I had a young man who was pretty much giving me everything I wanted and making sure I was good. He took good care of me.

I liked the way James took care of me. He wanted to make sure I was going to school, he wanted to make sure I ate well, and he wanted to make sure I looked nice. He knew my self-esteem was low; he did all that for me. I liked that because no one else cared for me like that. No one cared about my education, but he tried hard to make sure I would go to school.

My friends and I cut class all the time. We hung out at 102 Park; it was right next door to the police station. The police couldn't touch us or make us go back to school because it was a public park—we had the right to be there. We used to be out there partying, drinking, with loud music, dancing, and just chilling. I loved it because being there made me forget how I was feeling.

I started to hate school more and more. It was more fun for me to hang out with my friends, drink, and smoke. James' new job had people wanting to be around us more. Everybody knew Jimmy, and his new job was that he was a hustler—he sold drugs on the streets of Queens, NY, and I was his girl.

One day, I got into a fight at school. I was known for fighting. One of my friends called James without me knowing. Before I knew it, James and his crew were up at my school. They came up there to protect me and stand up for me. The word was out: don't mess with her—she's a fighter, and her man and his crew did not play. With James, I felt safe!

Chapter 9
The Streets Are Calling Us!

Now that my boyfriend was hustling, we were living our best lives. We were renting cars, driving around in stolen cars, going out to eat whatever we wanted, shopping—just blowing money. Life was good. I was 15 years old and wanted for nothing; life was carefree. James and I decided to take our relationship to the next level. I was nervous because sex was scary for me. My experience as a child was traumatic, and I had always associated sex with that trauma—it was all I knew. It turned out that my experience with James was different; he was always concerned about me and made sure I was okay. I did not expect that type of concern and love for me. In that experience, I felt the safest I have ever felt. All I could hear in my mind was the song by Stephanie Mills, "I Never Knew Love Like This Before." I was never lonely again. At 15, I knew I would spend the rest of my life with James. I never wanted that feeling to end. Three months later, I found out that I was pregnant. We discussed what we were going to do, and he said, "Whatever you decide to do, I will support you." Two weeks later, my life had a drastic change. My life as I knew it was turned upside down. James had been arrested and sent to Rikers Island. I was so lost—pregnant and alone—I didn't know what to do or what I was going to do. The young man who was taking care of me and my brothers was now locked up. Some of our friends knew I was pregnant, so they did their best to be there for me. I started having morning sickness, so I decided to tell my mother. Remember when I told you the story about my mother getting pregnant with me, and how Jamaicans don't believe in abortion? My mother said to me, "Shawn, you are only 15 years old, but whatever you decide to do, I will support

51

you." I knew she meant it with her whole heart, but with her drug addiction, I knew I wouldn't get much help. I could not take care of myself; how was I going to take care of a baby at 15? I made the worst decision of my life. I decided to get an abortion (I regret it to this day).

My mother took me to the abortion clinic, where there were so many young ladies of all races and ages. When we got there, there was a crowd of people protesting, yelling, and handing out literature. As we were walking up, a lady handed me a pamphlet. My mom said, "Don't take that," but I, my fast self, took it anyway.

As we got in the elevator, I took a glance and quickly closed the door—what I saw broke my heart. Mommy said, "I told you not to take it." I put my head down; I was so ashamed of what I saw and what I was about to do. I started to have 2nd thoughts; my mind was all over the place, and my emotions were on an all-time high. James was nowhere around for me to talk to him, so we couldn't decide together. My thoughts were: Would James hang around? Would I be a good mother? How could I love this baby when I couldn't even love myself? How could I not love something that James and I created? I didn't have a job—I was still in high school; I never went to class. What if what happened to me happens to my child?

A few minutes passed, and my mother turned to me, looked into my eyes, and said, "Shawnie, are you sure you want to do this?" That look I saw in my mother's eyes—I knew that if I said I wasn't going to do it, she was going to be there to help me raise my baby. I took a long, deep breath and said, "I'm sure," but my heart was yelling NO. I heard a loud voice say, "LaShawn, it's my turn." The walk down that hallway seemed like forever. It was cold and hollow, and my heart was beating so fast I felt like I couldn't catch my breath.

Finally, I reached a right turn. As I looked into the room, there was a bed and a gown. I was then instructed to put the gown on and lie on the bed with my feet in the stirrups. It seemed like everything was moving in slow motion.

The tears began to fall and roll down my face. I soaked my pillow with tears of pain; my heart was breaking over this awful thing I was doing. The nurse grabbed my hand, looked into my eyes, and said, "You will be okay." As she held and stroked my hand, fear overcame me—I was shaking so bad that she began to rub my hand.

I was thinking to myself, "How am I ever going to be okay? I'm killing my baby." My heart was breaking all over again. (I still regret it to this day.)

The doctor put a mask on my face and told me to count down from 10. The next thing I knew, my eyes were opening to see the same nurse. I remembered what had just happened and started crying all over again. I can't believe what I just did. OH MY GOODNESS, THE CRAMPS I HAVE! It was so painful, but the pain in my heart was worse.

I was in the house for days; I did not want to see anyone or do nothing. All I wanted was for James to come home and get out of jail. I went to James' friend—the guy he hustled for—to get him out and pay the bail. He assured me he was going to get him out.

A few hours later, James was home. Weeks passed, and our lives seemed to be back on track, you know, normal—doing what we do.

James was back on his game, and things started to pick up for us—the streets were still calling; we were about that life. That was all we knew at this point, and this was how we survived. One of our friends stole his dad's car, so we all loaded up in it. It was a station wagon, so you could imagine how full the car was.

We went joyriding, and we collectively decided to rob this man at gunpoint. James and I were like Bonnie & Clyde. We had done so much and experienced so much that when I think back on the things we done, I be like, "What in the world were we thinking?" (When I think back over my life, my soul cries Hallelujah.) The decisions we made meant we were not supposed to be here today to tell it.

I was now in the 10th grade for the 2nd time. Remember, I did tell you I was hanging out at the school more than I went to class. I was just doing me! The next day, I went up to the school to meet up with my crew. The day started off good— we even decided to go to class. As I was walking down the hallway, another crew was coming toward us. We did not get along, but we didn't bother each other. But on this day, one of the girls decided to bump into me real hard. So, I punched her in the face, and the brawl was on. Girls were fighting all over the place, and one boy jumped in—this was the boyfriend of the girl who started everything. I stood my ground and fought him; I did not care—I was going for broke.

The security guards came and broke everything up. In New York, schools usually had a task force on site—we even had a small police station on campus. When school let out, James and his boys were already up there. When I walked out, James walked up to me and asked, "Which dude was it?" I showed him, and James just walked up to the guy and knocked him out. All of that boy's friends jumped in, and the brawl began in front of the high school.

All of a sudden, the sound of sirens was heard. Everyone began to scatter, and we jumped in the car and were on our way. Then, all of a sudden, we noticed that James was bleeding—he had been stabbed. OMG, my boyfriend got stabbed in his chest. I was so scared. We were going to rush him to the hospital, but he ordered us not to. I was terrified. As we got close to home, James took his shirt off so we could examine his wound, and it wasn't too deep. God saved his life that day! (I wonder why?) Thank God.

James could've died that day protecting me. God protected him. I will share why God kept him later on: Psalms 121:5, "The LORD is thy keeper: the LORD is thy shade upon thy right hand."

The heat between us and them went on for weeks. I remember my cousin got his jaw broken in 3 places because of all this heat between us and them. It finally died down, and everyone went on with life as usual.

One night, I heard a knock at my door. It was a friend who was like my big brother—he and James were really good friends. When I opened the door, he was standing there, soaking wet, with a fur coat and all these bags.

The boy had robbed another drug dealer's house. They weren't home as he planned, but they came back early, so he jumped out the window with what he had, jumped into Jamaica Bay, and hid in the water for a while. When the coast was clear, he escaped and ran to my house.

We took all the money out of the money bag and laid it on the radiators, the floor, and the couches to dry out. We counted the money—it was so much. He gave me some cash—I won't say how much—but know it wasn't no little bit of change. He also gave me 2 gold chains and a bracelet.

Chapter 10
He Is Leaving Me Again!

The time came when James had to do time again; he was shipped to upstate NY to a program called S.H.O.C.K. It was still incarceration, but it was more like a boot camp. I remember traveling upstate NY to see him. The bus ride would take hours. I hated the time we spent apart. Back at home, our friends made sure I was good, but there was no replacement for James. I decided to get a job because the money was gone, and I had to maintain some sort of life that I was used to. I had gotten 2 gold teeth in my mouth, a gold ring on every finger, and my neck was full of chains. I was a Queen's girl for life. I got my first job at Wendy's. I really liked it—I was doing something other than the streets. I met new people and made new friends. It was different for me—a whole new world instead of the world I knew. James and I would keep in touch by writing letters, sending pictures, and talking on the phone. I hated when those calls ended, but there was something different about him. He would tell me about his daily activities and all he was learning there. James also received his GED while there. It snowed a lot up there, and those young men would be out there cutting down trees and doing all kinds of things. I think this was good for him; it exposed him to a whole new way of life. We both were exposed to a new way—maybe this would be good for both of us. This may change our minds about the street life. I often wondered what our future would be.

Chapter *11*
It's Graduation Day!

I picked out my outfit my outfit my nails were done, fresh box braids, leather jacket and fresh timberland boots—pink ones to be exact.

Ok, time to go to sleep; got a big day tomorrow. The alarm clock went off at 4:15, and we had to meet the bus to go upstate at 6am.

James was graduating from the S.H.O.C.K program.

The excitement was so overwhelming—just to think this would be my last ride upstate. This time, he will be sitting next to me on that bus going home.

My best friend was coming home, and things are going to be different for us.

The ceremony begins, and all you hear are Ten Hut Boutttt Face! All the young men marched in; my eyes were looking all over the place, but I couldn't find James anywhere.

My heart dropped. Where is he? OH God, did he get in trouble? Will he still be coming home?

All of a sudden, a young light-skinned guy lifted his head up—and it was him. He looked so different, with a low haircut; he was so disciplined, standing tall and confident.

The smile on my face would have told you everything.

My heart was beating like 1000 miles per second—I couldn't wait to wrap my arms around him.

Finally, the ceremony ended, and he was able to greet his mother, brother, and me.

When he wrapped his arms around me, the fragrance of Blue Nile cologne consumed me. It had me mesmerized.

It was time for us to load up on the bus and go home. I looked back at all the young men leaving with their families—it did my heart good. They all had a second chance to be on the right track.

We were home, and James's first task was to find a job. He had plenty of interviews, but no one seemed to want to give him a chance.

He had to remain in that positive state of mind, but it was very difficult for him when he heard no.

You know, on the job application there's a question that asks, "Have you ever been convicted of a felony?" Yeah, that question.

James answered yes, trying to be honest and upright.

Shortly after—about six months later—I found out that I was pregnant again. I started having morning sickness and missed my period.

So, I scheduled a doctor's appointment.

The doctor came in and said, "LaShawn, you are 12 ½ weeks pregnant." She then asked, "How do you feel about that?" I said, "Well, I'm only 17," so I never answered her question.

She then asked, "Is the baby's father in your life? Will he support you?" I answered, "Yes, he is."

The doctor also said, "You know, you have options." She handed me some information and mentioned that there is adoption and abortion.

I handed her back the information; I had already made up my mind that abortion was not an option.

I would never do that again. I was keeping my baby.

My mother and her siblings decided to sell Grandma's house, so we had to move.

Mommy found a house to rent in St Albans, Queens.

It was nice, but James and I would not be on the same block anymore.

I waited for James to come up the block to my house, but he was nowhere around.

I wanted to tell him what happened at the doctor's appointment. I waited and waited for James, and that was not like him.

I wondered if he figured it out and didn't want to have anything to do with me or the baby.

Where was he?

All of a sudden, I heard someone yelling "Mosquibo"—that was his nickname for me. Then I heard "oooh-oooh"; that was a call we did so all our friends would know we were outside.

So I went downstairs and opened the door. Of course, I was a little angry and upset, but I also felt nervous about having the conversation with James about the pregnancy and my decision to keep the baby.

James's parents were from Haiti and were a little strict; even though his father did not live there anymore, he still had a lot of say when it came to James and his brother. I know that his mom didn't care for me that much.

Honestly, I felt she did not think I was good enough for her son; I believe she wanted him with a pretty fair-skinned Haitian girl with long, pretty hair.

To me, his mother was bouchée.

I thought about my whole situation; it felt like I was reliving my mother's story when she was pregnant with me by my biological dad—how his mother and he acted with my mother.

I wondered: Would James's mother and father convince him not to be there for the baby and me, or convince him to talk me into getting an abortion—offering to pay for it—or would he stand up to them and tell them he was going to support me and our baby? I had so many questions running through my mind.

So, James and I continued our conversation, and I explained everything to him.

I waited for his response, and he said, "I will support you."

We decided that we were going to keep our baby, soon to become little Mrs. Janasia.

Chapter 12
It's Moving Day!

I told Mommy that I was pregnant and that I was keeping the baby.

Mommy didn't have much to say about it, as far as I can remember.

She was probably thinking to herself, "She's only 17."

I was very mature for my age and had been for a very long time.

I knew how to cook, clean, and keep house. I helped raise my brothers, so I knew how to prepare formula and change diapers—which to me meant having my baby wouldn't be that hard.

So, I thought!

We moved, and James helped us move.

He hung out there a lot; he would even stay the nights sometimes.

It wasn't the same as living up the block from him.

At that point, I had dropped out of high school; I had not made it past the 10th grade.

James started hanging out with his boys more, and I started to see less and less of him.

His time was being occupied by something else or someone else. I was now 5 ½ months pregnant and huge.

I ate all the time.

Gosh, when you hear people say you're eating for two, that's the truth.

James and I were talking, and I asked him if he had told his parents. He said no, and when I asked when he was going to tell them, he always said, "Soon." I responded, "Ok." Was he ashamed of me? My first thought was that he was always the worst in our crew. My best friend was the first one to have a baby by one of James's friends—we were still in high school then.

He was of Indian descent. They dated throughout high school, but when she became pregnant, his parents were going to disown him if he stayed with her. He actually broke up with her right after the baby was born; she was heartbroken.

I was about 6 months pregnant by then, and James and I were off and on. He still came over when he wanted to and sometimes spent the nights. He was my baby daddy, so in my eyes, we were still together. It seemed like it was okay for him to do whatever he wanted, but when it came to me, he wouldn't listen. Crazy, right? Double standard!

My Mother was working in Manhattan. I had an appointment in Manhattan that day, so I went to her job so we could ride the train home together. I was sitting at her desk, eating Oreo cookies that tasted like the best Oreos I had ever eaten.

I suddenly felt the urge to use the restroom. As I left the

restroom and began to walk back up the hallway, I felt a slight gush of water. I kept walking, and then water was everywhere around my feet. OMG, my water just broke! Two ladies were there, and they said, "OMG, your water just broke!" They ran to get my Mother and called 911.

I was not having contractions, but I was really scared. I asked my mother to try to reach James—of course, no response. We arrived at the hospital; the plan was to try to make me hold the baby as long as I could, but the risk was that there could be an infection for me and the baby because there was no water. I still hadn't heard anything from my baby's father. Twenty-four hours later, I started to get a fever—that meant there was an infection from holding the baby without water. All I could think was, "Where was he? I'm going through this by myself; where is he?" My mom had to go home to my two little brothers.

The doctor came in to check my cervix and stated that the baby was shaking her hand—Janasia was sticking her arm out—so they had to do a c-section to get her out. Janasia was born December 23, 1991; she was born three months prematurely. It was now December 24th, Christmas Eve. Guess who walked through the door? Yup, you guessed it—it was James. He sat for a while; he saw Nasia. He said, "She's so little, and she is…" James left shortly after while he had family in from Boston for the holidays.

I was all alone in the hospital on Christmas—just me and Nasia. No one came to see me on Christmas. The only joy I had was going to see my baby in the NICU; she was the most beautiful little creation I had ever laid eyes on. Wow, I was a mother—someone I could love and someone who would love me back unconditionally.

As the nurse wheeled me back to my room, tears fell. I loved that little baby so much, and she loved me. We spent Christmas together at St. Vincent Hospital in Manhattan, NY. It was time for me to go home, but Janasia had to stay there for almost three months until she weighed five pounds. Finally, it was time for us to bring her home. James and I were going to take the train home, but my daddy called and said he would take us to pick her up.

I had not spoken to him in months. When I told Daddy I was having a baby, he got really upset and stopped talking to me.

Janasia was born. Now, I guess he got over it—she was here, and that was his grandbaby. I know it was hard for him that his baby girl had a baby, but I was doing me.

Daddy still did not know. I knew the truth—that he wasn't my biological dad—but to me, he was my daddy; no one could ever change that.

James and Daddy put Nasia's crib together.

My dad was so mean to James that he didn't have much to say—there was hardly any conversation. I prayed that one day that would change.

James would come over and spend time with Janasia and me, but things were not like they used to be. I lived way across town, and James was doing his own thing. Time went by, and I thought to myself, "I need my own money and a job—but who would hire a teenage mom with no high school diploma? Was I going to live with my mother forever?" So, I decided to enroll in the G.E.D. program and received my high school diploma in March of 1992.

Chapter 13
New Beginnings!

James' parents decided they were going to send him to nursing school. I was really excited for him and for us. I knew that one day James would be my husband, even when he didn't know. I thought that James would become a nurse and we would get our own place and be one happy family.

He started nursing school, and he seemed to like it. He began meeting new people and making new friends, all without me. It seemed like there was no room for me in that part of his life.

I had to do something to occupy my time and to make some money. Since he was in school, he stopped hustling. I got a job at the local supermarket as a cashier, and I also began meeting new people. I even had a side hustle doing hair. My clientele began to pick up when I started doing the famous French rolls that were my signature style and updo's. I started making some change.

James and I were still in some sort of relationship—for what it was worth—but it just wasn't the same. But he was my baby daddy, and I loved him. I started getting more and more clients of all nationalities, and I began making new friends myself.

James started keeping Janasia on the weekends with him. That meant free time for me. Yesssssssss, it was nice to have time to myself and a whole new group of friends to hang out with—both male and female.

One weekend, I was over at James' house when the phone

rang. I answered it, and on the other end, a voice said, "Hello, can I speak to James?"

I said, "Sure, who's calling?" I wanted to know who the chic was on the other end calling my boyfriend. She said _____. I kindly said to him, "Here so and so is calling for you." I sat right there and listened to the whole conversation. When he hung that phone up, y'all know what happened next, right? Hurricane Shawn came through, and after that, I was livid. I grabbed my stuff, left Janasia there, and I was out. I called my cab and left. The person who I thought would never break my heart did. So that's why your time is so occupied—you busy entertaining this other chick. Ok, so I see now. I think she may have stolen his heart. The girl on the other end was a pretty Haitian girl with long hair, exactly what his mom wanted for him. I had so many questions. Was I too ugly? Was I just a girl from his past who wouldn't make it to his future? Was I a nobody? I just wasn't good enough. I was so insecure; she was so pretty. We did not break up. I loved him. I felt like he was the only one who had really been there for me, and I did not want to give up on us. Even though I was hurt, I still felt he would marry me one day. Was this false hope? My self-esteem was already low, but I felt this made it worse.

I was lonely cause now he had school, new friends, and he was entertaining some other girl. He thought I didn't know he was still talking to her, but I knew. There was an older guy around my neighborhood who was interested in me. He was about 4 years older than me.

For a long time, I paid him no attention, but the more James stayed away, the more my attention went to the guy who was giving me attention. We used to sit on my porch and have long talks. He knew about James. He used to hustle, and every time I went to the store across the street from my house, he was there.

One day, I went into the store and he said, "I haven't seen homeboy around." All I could say was, "Yeahhh." I placed my items on the counter—milk, diapers, and groceries. He paid the bill for me and carried my stuff across the street.

He said something to me. He said, "I want to get to know you better, but I know you're still attached to old boy," but he didn't care. The next thing he said, I was like, "My life is changing." He said, "I can take care of you and your daughter. You would want for nothing." Then he said, "You should go back to school," and he asked, "What do you want out of life?" I really had no answers.

As months went on, he and I hung out more and more. James visited every now and then. One thing my new friend never did was disrecpoot me. If he knew James was there, he wouldn't come over, knock on my door, or nothing. He was there for me, so I wanted for nothing. We never crossed that line—even though we could've—because he respected my wishes.

One day, he came over and said he was moving to Long Island—he was buying a house. He had a lot of money from hustling, plus his mom passed away and left him and his brother a lot of money. His brother was going to stay in the house they grew up in, but he wanted to buy his own, so he did.

He and I were talking, and he said, "I care about you." I laughed because I thought it wasn't true. After the stuff with James, I wasn't in the business of trusting any guys. We sat and talked, and he asked me to move in with him. He said, "Janasia, I would be set, and I'll take care of us." It sounded good, but he wasn't James.

My friend was going to move in about a month and a half. A week before he moved, he came by and asked me again. I told him, "No, I couldn't do it; I still loved James." I thanked him for being there for me. He said, "You could always have this." Then he said, "I'll be right back." He went up the street to his house and returned with a few bags. In one bag was a jacket and some sneakers for me; in the second bag were some sneakers for Janasia and a jacket. I thought that was so sweet.

I gave him a hug. He said, "Here is my new number—call me if you ever need anything. If old boy (James) messes up, I'm there to pick up the pieces." I gave him a hug, and he added, "Old boy (James) don't know how lucky he is." That was the last time I saw my friend; I never called him. I wondered, "Did I miss my opportunity for a better life?"

Chapter 14
What Am I Supposed To Do Now?

My mom sprung some news on me: we were moving uptown to Manhattan. We were moving to Harlem, one building down from my aunt and cousins. Now, this was further from James—this was in a whole different borough, about an hour ride on the A train. Janasia was about 2 years old now. Harlem was so different from Queens; there was so much fashion, so many beauty salons, and so many barber shops. 125th Street was about 10 minutes from us, and the Apollo Theater too. Most people my age had their own apartments and were living the life. My cousins and all their friends were rocking fur coats and all kinds of jewelry. Oh yeah, I think I'm going to like it here. Harlem is it.

James must have had a change of heart because he was coming to Harlem every weekend. I was coming and going as I pleased—at this point, I was really living my own life. I did whatever I wanted to do. We would sleep all afternoon, then get up in the evening, shower, get dressed, and just go sit on the block. We would be out there till the late hours of the night, drinking and smoking weed. Music would be blasting outside.

My aunt used to cook and sell plates—the best soul food you would ever taste. Everybody on the block got food from her. I was 19 and living the Ghetto fabulous life. All of the guys had some kind of hustle going on, and most of the young ladies stayed fly, but living on the system (welfare)—free money, food stamps, rent paid, and free groceries. Those days, everybody did something in Harlem—whether it was smoking weed, sniffing cocaine, or smoking cocaine and drinking. I did drink and smoke weed; did my drug use go further? Thank God, no it did not. Being that my mother was addicted, I did not want to do that to myself or my children. That curse was going to stop with me.

My baby daddy was making money again because after he graduated nursing school, they would not allow him to take the test to become a nurse because of his previous felony charges. I applied for this program called Section 8, and I was called for a program that was a part of Section 8 called J.I.T.T.E.R.S. It was Section 8, but the rules were a little different. It was time for me to get my own place. I finally got my own spot on 150th Street and St. Nicholas. I was so happy—I finally had my own apt; now my man could move in with me, and we would be good. James gave me money to furnish the whole apt—it was so nice. James stayed up there all the time, but didn't really live there.

He had clothes—a lot of his stuff—uptown with me, but he had to be at home because his parents weren't having that. He stayed uptown for one whole week until his dad came calling, telling him to go home. I was like, "Dag, you grown." Did he go home? NOPE, he stayed another week. Finally, he decided to go back to Queens. He left on Sunday and was back uptown Friday to be with me and his daughter. I would cook dinner and bring him his plate.

We would just lay up, chill, and smoke on our fire escape. We'd sit out there and just watch all that was going on in the streets of Harlem.

My friend hooked me up with a job as a receptionist where she worked, and the boss would pay me cash under the table so my welfare benefits wouldn't stop. I worked Monday through Friday, 8 AM to 5 PM. After work on Fridays, the team would meet my boss at the bar for drinks.

I also would pick up my pay, and then sometimes he would throw in a little extra shoot, which was okay for me. My job was downtown Manhattan. I dressed up professionally every day, and this was really my first experience working a professional job and with white professional people. I liked it, and it was a new experience for me. James was there with Nasia some days. I paid my aunt to babysit when James was in Queens. Money was rolling in—he was making money, I was making money, and we had no bills.

When James was home uptown, his friends would come out there to hang out sometimes, and they did what they did, and I would cook for everybody. I remember when they first saw me bring James his plate, they were like, "Wifey, take care of you." The only thing was I was not his wife, but that's what they called long-term girlfriends at that time—wifey.

One weekend, James and I threw a party we called the Get Ripped Party. We moved all our furniture out of the apartment downstairs to my friend's apartment. We brought two big party speakers, and the DJ was killing it. There were bottles everywhere—all kinds of alcohol. We drank and danced all night. The next day, we woke up, and people were lying everywhere; blankets and people filled the floor. I remember there was someone sleeping in my tub—it was bananas. This party went down in history; people still talk about it to this day.

Chapter 15

Not Again

OMG! This is happening again—why, right when we were doing so good? Well, not good, but we thought we were good: two young people living the life. James got arrested and was locked up again for selling drugs. At this point, this was all we knew and had become accustomed to. He was providing for us the best way he knew how. We ate what we wanted, we wore what we wanted, we just blew money—and that was fun to us. It's crazy when you're in that life; you never think or imagine that the money won't be there until it's too late. My mother used to hang out at a bar called The Love Nest. She would be in there for days, coming out not even knowing what day it was.

My aunt was a barmaid there, and they spent most of their time there—people would come out like zombies. Sometimes my grandpa had to go in to get her out. Eventually, I guess mommy was tired and needed a change. Mommy packed up my two little brothers and moved to North Carolina.

James got out on bail, but his case took a long time with him going back and forth to court. His attorney was taking it to trial, so they kept getting continuances for the case.

Even though he was going back and forth to court, this did not stop him. We took advantage of mommy moving down south, and we started visiting her and my brothers. We had a connect down there already that we knew from NY, so we would always bring work back 95 north. James' case did not go that well—when he found out how much time he was facing, he did not want Nasia and me by ourselves, and I did not want him to go away again.

So, guess what we did? We went on the run to North Carolina to start a new life and get away from the drug game. They gave him a date to turn himself in.

I went down because he couldn't go. Yet, he found us an apartment—a townhouse close to my mother. I thought it was a good neighborhood. Then I came back up north, we got a moving truck, packed all of our stuff, and hit 95 south. It was so country to me—so slow—but maybe that was what we needed.

Our townhouse was on a street called Bragg Street. I knew nothing about this place; it looked nice to me and was nothing like New York, but at least we were together. The hood in North Carolina was nothing like the hood in New York, so I thought we were good. We were a modern-day Bonnie & Clyde.

James found a job, and I was hired as a team lead at a fast-food restaurant called Hardees. The work James did was labor work—he was paid cash by the day. We thought things were good and that things were gonna be different: new state, new life. That was not the case. When the Devil has a plan for you, he will do whatever he has to do to get you off focus. The thing is, change only comes when you make it up in your mind that you truly want change. Your mindset has to change. Lo and behold, the Devil was here in North Carolina waiting for us. He presented all the familiarities of street life. The Devil's job is to still, kill, and destroy. If James and I did keep it up, we would find ourselves in jail, dead.

James hooked up with some friends from NY who were in NC building a drug organization. Well, what do you think happened? He started his drug game all over again. Dacian Road in Raleigh was where they took over—the guys who used to run that area were wondering who these Up North cats were, coming down here trying to run Raleigh. That is exactly what James and his crew did—they took over.

I was downstairs in the kitchen cooking, waiting for James to come home, when all of a sudden I heard a lot of commotion. It was James and his friend running through the door. Then I heard a loud noise—BANG! BANG! —gunshots. I grabbed Janasia, ran upstairs, and got under the bed. James and his crew turned over my brand new CREAM leather couch to block them; they couldn't reach their weapons, which were in a closet that wasn't close to them.

That was it for me. James never allowed business to follow him home, but it did that night. My baby girl was there when all this was taking place; that was it for me.

We lived there for 8 months, but it was not safe, we had to go. Our landlord had another house for rent. It cost a little more, but it was so much better—it was huge, and I loved it. We had 3 bedrooms, a kitchen, a living room with a fireplace, and a dining room. We rented that for $500.

It was probably about 2 months later that James' parents began to call because he missed the court date where he was to turn himself in. They called for months. His dad didn't know exactly where we were, but his mother did know that my mom lived in Raleigh, NC. Finally, they convinced him to come back and do his time.

I was still working at Hardees, training for a position as assistant manager. When James left, my heart was broken. Am I going to experience a broken heart for the rest of my life? I did not want to stay in that big house by myself, so my brother and cousin pretty much moved in with me. They got on my nerves—they were two young guys who don't cook or clean.

My mother had been clean from drugs and alcohol for several years now. Mommy had gotten introduced to Jesus Christ and was now saved and in church. Oh, and she was married and 5 months pregnant.

Chapter 16

Ughhhhhh!!!!!

What is going on? I feel awful. Is it because I'm tired? Maybe I was working too much. I just don't feel good. I'm trying to move fast, but I'm moving so slow. I made it to the bathroom and I threw up. Maybe I ate something bad at work, I dunno, or maybe I got a stomach virus. I know I'm not pregnant—I did not miss my cycle. Four days later, I'm still throwing up, so I figured at this point I better see a doctor.

I went to the appointment, and the doctor comes in. He looks at me and says, "LaShawn... you have a case of—" I was so scared I had no clue what he was about to say next. Then he said, "You're pregnant." I was shocked. I guess in about eight months I'm gonna have a baby.

I wrote to James and told him, and he was happy—just sorry he wasn't there with me. Four months later, I found out we were having a little boy. I hadn't been up north to see James in a while—I was working so much and getting huge. I was lazy and didn't feel like taking those long train rides to NY and then a bus ride upstate, but Nasia had been asking, "When is my daddy coming home from big people college?"—that's what we had told her.

A few months later, I gave birth to a full-term baby boy. We named him Justin; he was born May 3rd, 1996. I waited until Justin was one month old and planned a trip to NY so his daddy could meet him. James' mother and grandmother were excited to meet Justin too.

The phone rang. The person on the other end said, "You have a collect call from an inmate at a NY state correctional facility. Before it could ask if you accept, press 1." I already pressed 1.

I told James we were coming up to visit. I packed up my two children and got on Amtrak. We were in two seats—it was okay until we had to change trains. When we arrived in Virginia, one of the employees must have seen how tired and frustrated I was. She asked, "Where are you traveling to?" I answered, "NY." Then she said, "Come up to the counter, sweetheart," so I did.

When I walked up to the counter, she said to me, "I am going to upgrade your ticket." I really did not know what the upgrade meant—I just thought it was a better seat. When I boarded the train, I was looking for my seat. Another employee saw how confused I was and asked to see my ticket. He then said, "Come this way."

We arrived at a door. He pushed it open, and it was a huge room with a TV, bathroom, and a huge bed. The big window in the room was nice. I was so Thankful! Favor ain't Fair!

We finally made it to Manhattan. I took the train to Queens, then caught a taxi to James' mom's house. I rang the bell; she opened the door and was happy to see the kids. She grabbed Justin out of my arms and grabbed Nasia by the hand, and we walked into the living room.

The next morning, we met the bus to go upstate. James was so happy to see us. Nasia ran up to him and yelled, "Daddy!" He looked at me and winked—my heart melted. He walked over to me and gave me the biggest hug and kiss, then he looked at Justin; his eyes were stuck on his son for a minute. We sat down at the table and enjoyed our visit.

Wow, James and I had two children. Maybe now, since I gave

him a son, he would make me his wife. The time had come for us to leave. My heart was crushed—I cried; I missed my best friend. I was his rider; I told him a long time ago that I would always be there for him, and I meant that. He hugged me so tight that I held on to him for as long as I could. James kissed his two children, and we left.

As I turned back around, we met eyes. He nodded at me and then winked. I made a decision then: I wanted to be closer to him so I could visit him more. James wanted us closer, so he asked his mother if I could move into his old room. There was no hesitation that I know of—her immediate answer was yes.

I told my mother I was moving back to NY. She did not want us to go, but she understood, plus her house was getting too crowded. She had my two brothers and my baby sister, then me and my two children—it was time for me to go. I guess NC wasn't it for us. Why did we think being on the run could be a normal or good life for us? Young and dumb!

I had to find a job to take care of my children. I found a job at Checkers fast food restaurant. I started as a regular crew member, but two weeks later they started to train me as a shift manager, and eventually I was promoted to assistant manager.

I had been working for them for about 2 years—almost 3 years. James was coming home soon; I just did not know when. During that time, I started hanging out a lot. James' mother watched the kids, and sometimes I worked until about midnight. I worked in Long Island, and I started meeting new people, plus I hooked back up with all my old crew.

I started meeting new guys who were interested in me. The thing back then was, they always asked, "You gotta man?" I would say yes, and they would ask, "Where he at?" I would say, "Locked up," and they took that as an opportunity to try and talk to me. I wasn't feeling that.

I saved up enough money to purchase me a car—I had a 1987 navy blue Ford Taurus. My letters and visits to James became less and less; my time was occupied with my life and what I had going on.

After work, my friends from Hempstead would go hang out. We would go to one of the girls' houses, shower, get dressed, and hit the clubs. I was basically living out of my car; I kept extra clothes in my trunk.

One of my friends from Brooklyn needed a job, so I got her on at Checkers. She was seeing this guy from my neighborhood—he was from Brooklyn, but he was now living out there with his kids' mother. It was three girls and their two guy friends—I was by myself. The guys had a friend they started bringing around—it was a set-up.

He had a slick mouth, always having something smart to say—he kinda got on my nerves. Then he started popping up at my job, sending flowers. I was like, "uh uh, my baby daddy coming home soon," and he was like, "when?" I still did not know the exact time frame. He said, "Well, he's lost. He shouldn't have left you out here by yourself." He was like, "There are wolves out here." Next, he said, "Give me a chance." I looked down at this man's hand—he had a ring on his finger—and I yelled, "BOY, YOU'RE MARRIED!" I said, "Conversation over." He said, "Wait, wait—we separated; I'm getting ready to move out." He was a hustler, him and his boys—it seemed like I couldn't get these drug dealer men away. I guess I always felt they could give me what I needed or wanted. I said, "Okay, you can leave now." He said, "What time you get off?" I said, "About 1:30 AM." He said, "Okay, that boy did not go nowhere." He came back up to the window, ordered food, and said, "I'm not going nowhere. I'm going to wait till you get off and make sure you get home safe." He parked at my job for hours. I finally was off, and when I came out the door, he had a single rose for me and opened my car door. I got in, we drove off; he followed me until we reached the Van Wyck, then he went his way and I went on my way. What is happening? Is this guy pulling my attention away from the man I loved? The next day, I went to work and he did not pop up. I was cool with that, 'cause the feeling I had was scary. Could there actually be someone that can pull my heart from James? Actually, he had come up there before I got there. He dropped off a card and another single rose. I opened the card and there was a little message in there, but there was also $500 cash in the card that said, "Buy yourself something nice." I had not seen him for a couple of days.

He had not paged me either; I just figured him and his wife decided to make up and stay together. One day, out of the blue, him and his friends pulled up to my job to see me and my friends. He asked if we could talk. I was like, "Cool, give me a few—I'll take a break." When I came outside, he said, "I know you haven't seen me in a while, but I want to tell you: me and my wife have decided to try to work it out." I was like, "Cool, I understand." I said to him, "I will be ok; my baby daddy be home soon, so I did not want to get serious." He was like, "I want us to still talk. I want you in my life, but I wanna be with her too. Boy, you nutzzzz—I'm young but I ain't dumb by no means." He said, "I don't care about you, baby daddy." I said, "You should be." He stated he was going to steal me from James. No way that would happen—I was tapped in for life. We still kept in touch 'cause him and his crew would hang out at my job. I started liking him even more; he would not disappear.

My car broke down, and he got it towed to James' mother's house and then sent a mechanic to fix it. Two weeks later, to my surprise, a car pulled up—it was James' friend's car. The passenger door opened, and who jumped out? My man was home! I was so excited but nervous at the same time. "Please don't let these dudes pull up while James is here—that would not be good." I paged the guy to let him know, "Don't come to my job." Our communication at this point had to come to a cease.

Somehow, detective James got a hold of my pager and listened to the message from the guy. He was soooooooooooooo mad and hurt—I guess he knows what it feels like when someone is trying to steal the heart of the person you love. James took my pager and threw it out the window and crushed it. There was a boxing match after that. We were something! Two hotheads trying to stand their ground. I loved him and he loved me. We made up, and life went on...

Finally

It was 3 months later—I was now 25 years old, and James and I had 2 children, Janasia and Justin. James asked me to be his wife. The proposal went a little something like this:

James: Yo, we gonna do this or what?

Me: Do what?

James: Get Married!

Me: Yessssssssssssssssss!

I called my mom, and the wedding planning began. Finally, after all we had been through—the ups and the downs, the highs and lows—a Queens love story still lasts. I was going to be Mrs. James Sam. James said, "Once we get married, we're moving down south." So I did my wifely duties and got all James' parole stuff transferred to NC. We planned our wedding for September 5, 1998. We planned that wedding in 6 months— my dress was paid for, the caterer had been chosen, and we reserved a stretch Lincoln Navigator for the wedding party. The bridesmaids and groomsmen had been chosen, and dresses and tux were picked out. It was finally happening—I was going to marry the love of my life. I was so happy; dreams really do come true.

I asked myself, "God, were you finally working out things in my life? You never came through for me before. Are you working it out for me now?" I did not know God or understand anything about Him. All my experiences with this God seemed as though it was not in my favor, so I thought:

"For I know the plans I have for you," declares the LORD, "plans to prosper you and not to harm you, plans to give you hope and a future."— Jeremiah 29:11 New International Version

The wedding day was here. I walked down that aisle and married my best friend. "I Do" are two words I will never forget. We danced all night with friends and family. The reception was so big—our wedding party was a total of 24. Our guests were all dressed up in all kinds of colors. What do you expect? A room full of Hattians and Jamaicans—it was colorful. My cousin used to work for the Italians (the Mafia). They had a huge restaurant. He came in with trays and trays of food from the restaurant, on top of the food we had catered. I remember dancing with him; he turned the whole reception out. One year later, he was murdered. I miss him and will never forget him dancing at James and my wedding. RIP, Big Kev. The Sam wedding will go down in history. People still talk about that wedding to this day.

In December of 1998, we moved from NY to Raleigh, NC. This time, it was done the right way. We were no longer in the drug game, and we really wanted a new start. We were legit this time and not on the run. We were a little more mature now and wanted better for ourselves and our children. James' parole had been transferred to NC. Janasia was already in North Carolina; she had gone down after the wedding to start school. Janasia did not know we were coming because Christmas was near and it was her birthday, so we surprised her by moving to North Carolina.

We settled in, and things were good. We lived with my mom for a little while. Then we got our own apartment—it was so nice. It was about 1500 sq feet, with 3 bedrooms and a balcony.

It was amazing; there was even a pool. It was such a nice place. I found a job, and I tried to get James a job at the place where I worked, but they did a drug test, and he did not pass. He had smoked some weed, and the test came back positive, so they let him go.

After that, James and I began to argue a lot. I got a new job paying a whole lot more, and James was hanging out a lot. I was frustrated and, in the arguments, I would say some mean things—I would say things to belittle him—but I loved him. Did me yelling, screaming, or going off help? Was it right? NO, it was not. One thing I did not understand was that James was the head of the household, and I was his wife. Men don't like it when their women talk down to them.

Every time we argued, I would be so mean and then withhold sex from him. But let me give you some wisdom, ladies: what you don't do, another woman will. The Bible is the best teacher for a woman to be a wife. I was not humble now that was because of all my issues and stuff I had been through.

The Bible says in Ephesians 5:22-24 (King James Version):

22 Wives, submit yourselves unto your own husbands, as unto the Lord.

23 For the husband is the head of the wife, even as Christ is the head of the church: and he is the savior of the body.

24 Therefore as the church is subject unto Christ, so let the wives be to their own husbands in everything.

Back then, I knew nothing about the Bible—you know, it's funny. I wish I knew then what I know now. It doesn't matter, ladies; whether you make more money or not, your husband is still the head of the household. If your voice is louder, that doesn't make you the head. It doesn't say that if you save money and he doesn't, then you're the head. James and I were not getting along at all. He started staying out more and more. Come to find out, I was pregnant again, and we were so distant from one another. Time had passed—I was 5 months pregnant. One morning, I went to the bathroom and lost my mucus plug, but did not realize what was going on. So, I flushed and kept it moving.

I was so stressed out, and my man and I did not like each other very much, but we loved each other even in our dislike. My cousins wanted to get me out of the house. My mom had Nasia and Justin, so we went to my friend's house because I had started having some pains. The pain started coming faster and faster. They called 911, and the ambulance came and took me to UNC Chapel Hill Hospital. They had to do an emergency C-section—I was only 23 weeks; it was too early. I was so scared. I started to cry, and my husband was not there. They said, "We must do this now." Everyone was moving so fast—the doctors, the nurses—everyone was talking amongst themselves. They put the oxygen mask on me and told me to count down. I said, "10." That's all I remember.

The next thing I knew, I woke up in the recovery room. Then they took me to my room. I fell asleep, and when I woke up, I looked to the left—James was sitting there.

We named the baby Jaiden. Her dad and I went to the Neonatal Intensive Care Unit (NICU) to see her. She was so little.

About two weeks passed, and the doctors wanted to meet with James and me. We walked into the room—there was a team of doctors. As we sat down at the table, I saw a tissue box in the middle. My stomach started to knot up. *What are they getting ready to tell us?* I looked at their faces—the men showed no emotion, but some of the women, I could tell, felt for me because they knew what I was about to hear.

One male doctor began to speak, and this is what he said:

"Mr. and Mrs. Sam, your daughter was born very early. Some of her organs did not develop. Her lungs have pocket holes in them. You remember, Mrs. Sam, I told you there was a chance she would not make it through the night—but she did. However, she has also developed a bleed on her brain."

As the doctor explained, the tears began to fall.

"The fluid that circles around her spine is not moving properly."

I was like, God, what else?!

Then came the hardest part.

"She will not be able to hear or see, feed herself, walk, or do anything. She will not live past 30 days."

Thirty days later, Jaiden Yvonne Sam died in my arms.

This was the hardest thing I had ever been through. She looked so beautiful—she had a little white dress with a white headband. That day, I lost a part of me. Even now, it still brings tears to my eyes.

It was time for a change.

We were invited to church by my cousin. I walked through the door of this little church in a basement. That's the day my new life began.

God has a plan.

God has a plan for us even when we don't have a plan for ourselves. Stay tuned and see what God has planned for James and me. I had never trusted God since I was a child, but He brought me right back to Him.

This was different for me. But would this be what would heal me and my marriage?

Can I be healed from all my trauma?

A person who does not know how to show love. I wondered if God could teach me to love after not trusting love?

Stay tuned to see what God has in store.

What does the future hold for the Sams?

Jeremiah 29:11 (King James Version)

"For I know the thoughts that I think toward you, saith the Lord, thoughts of peace, and not of evil, to give you an expected end."

The Change has started! To be continued!

Meet the
Author

LaShawn Sam

LaShawn Sam was born and raised in Jamaica (Southside) Queens, NY. She is the wife of Pastor James Sam, with whom she co-labors at J. Sam Ministries. Together, they have four amazing children— Janasia (33), Justin (29), Jordan (23), and Josiah (12)—as well as one wonderful grandson, Carter, who is 4 months old. They now reside in North Carolina.

LaShawn holds a **Bachelor of Science in Business Administration** with a concentration in **Organizational Management.** She is currently working toward her **Master's degree in Health Administration.**

She is the visionary behind her non-profit, **Diamonds in God's Eyes,** which is dedicated to supporting little girls and women who have experienced sexual trauma. It is her passion to help individuals break free from carrying trauma through life.

"I have overcome, and I know you can overcome too. Trauma should not dictate your path in life—you tell trauma who you are and who you are going to be."

LaShawn mentors women of all ages and from all walks of life, reminding them that they are great and that **self-love is one of the best gifts you can give yourself.** However, **forgiving the trespasser is the most powerful gift**—this is what started her own healing process.